PRAYING *the* ATTRIBUTES *of* GOD

Rosemary Jensen

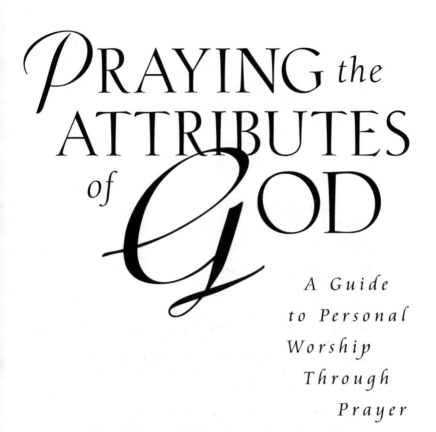

PRAYING *the* ATTRIBUTES *of* GOD

A Guide
to Personal
Worship
Through
Prayer

Rosemary Jensen

Kregel
Publications

Praying the Attributes of God: A Guide to Personal Worship Through Prayer

© 2002 by Rosemary Jensen

Published by Kregel Publications, P.O. Box 2607, Grand Rapids, MI 49501.

Library of Congress Cataloging-in-Publication Data
Jensen, Rosemary.
  Praying the attributes of God: a guide to personal worship through prayer / by Rosemary Jensen.
       p.   cm.
     1. God—Attributes—Meditations. 2. Prayers. I. Title

BT130 .J45   2002
242'.8—dc21   2002006249

ISBN 0-8254-2942-0

Printed in the United States of America

04 05 06 / 5 4 3

CONTENTS

CONTENTS

FOREWORD

It is possible for even Christians to take for granted the presence and greatness of God. We are often beset by distractions, with our work and with the demands of life. Indeed, such are our preoccupations that it is possible to attend worship services, sing the songs, hear the sermons, and leave, still unmindful of the greatness and grace of God.

But Christ summons us to live a God-centered and God-focused life. This is not a burden that weighs us down and bends our backs. Quite the reverse. Nothing is so liberating as the knowledge of God. It liberates us from the incessant tyranny of our own selves, from the captivity to the follies that assault us in the workplace, in the movies, and on television, demanding that we fall into line if we are to be regarded as "normal." It liberates us to find the original purpose of our creation, to see beyond what is immediate, urgent, and pressing to what is actually important and enduring. It is this knowledge that gives to life depth, integrity, direction, and stability amidst all of the storms and catastrophes.

I, therefore, welcome Rosemary Jensen's book because it is a useful guide in helping us to think about God, to seek after him in prayer, and to nurture in our lives the spiritual priorities that should result because of who God is. It is in thinking about him in his greatness, in the full array of his attributes, that our minds are enlarged, our lives are reoriented, and our thirst for him is deepened.

The psalmist, who knew so much less than we know about God's disclosure of himself in Scripture, nevertheless likened the longing of his soul for God to that of the deer who thirsts "for streams of water" (Ps. 42:1). May our thirsting for God be like that!

DAVID F. WELLS
Andrew Mutch Distinguished Professor
of Historical and Systematic Theology
Gordon-Conwell Theological Seminary

INTRODUCTION

*H*ow can anyone write a book about the very character of God? The truth is, I didn't start out to write a book at all. It just happened.

When, at age sixteen, I came to faith in Christ, God put into my heart the desire to teach others about him. At seventeen I knew I wanted to teach others in the foreign mission field. I didn't know enough about God, however, to teach anybody! But I did know that the Bible is the source of knowledge about God.

So I began a program of daily Bible reading that has persisted throughout my life.

That habit only heightened my desire to know God more fully. John 17:3 says that eternal life consists of knowing God and his Son Jesus Christ. So I set a goal to read through the entire Bible and write out the verses that exemplify or explain God's attributes. As the list of attributes grew, I decided to stop at thirty-one and focus on one attribute a day as I worshiped God for a month.

I spent more than three years reading and writing the verses. Going over the verses month after month, I learned much about God—knowledge that I could pass on to others. As Executive Director of Bible Study Fellowship (BSF), I shared these verses with the staff and leadership and was encouraged by their response.

But more importantly, my knowledge of God led me to praise and give thanks each day as, through the actual words of

Scripture, I meditated on his specific attributes. As I concentrated on God himself, the Holy Spirit led my prayers of petition to be more God-centered. And I prayed that others would benefit from knowing God in these specific ways.

The format of *Praying the Attributes of God* is that of the acrostic ACTS (adoration, confession, thanksgiving, and supplication), and I believe its primary value lies in personal devotions. It would also be good to use as an annual prayer diary. This is not a "how to" book. It is designed so that the words from Scripture sink into your mind and then into your heart. The Holy Spirit will then lead you into the action he wants you, as an individual, to take.

At present this material is being used where The Rafiki Foundation operates vocational training centers for teenage girls in developing countries. Each morning for half an hour, these girls learn to know God through the Scriptures, to confess their sins to him, to thank him, and to pray to him. My prayer is that as a result, their lives will be changed.

All proceeds from the sale of this book will go to the operation of these Rafiki centers.[1]

I am grateful to my family and the staff of Rafiki and BSF for their encouragement. In particular, I thank Mary Ann Oatis, a BSF teaching leader who insisted that this book be published—and went to the trouble to see that it was.

The book is dedicated to my husband, Bob, who has always encouraged me to fulfill God's calling and provided me with his love and support in doing so.

My prayer for you, the reader, is that, as you use this book, you too will be filled with the love of God and the knowledge of his fullness.

---

[1] For more information, write The Rafiki Foundation, 19001 Huebner Road, #2, San Antonio, TX 78258; or, www.rafiki-foundation.org.

PRAYING *the* ATTRIBUTES *of* GOD

1

ACCESSIBLE

Adoration

Deuteronomy 4:7: What other nation is so great as to have *Moses.*
their gods near them the way the LORD <u>our God is near us</u>
<u>whenever we pray to him?</u>

Psalm 27:4: One thing I ask of the LORD, this is what I seek: *David*
that I may dwell in the house of the LORD all the days of my
life, to gaze upon the beauty of the LORD and <u>to seek him</u> in
his temple.

Matthew 6:6: When you pray, go into your room, close the *Jesus.*
door and ~~pray~~ *talk* to your Father, who is <u>unseen.</u> Then your
Father, who sees what is done in secret, will reward you.

John 14:6: Jesus answered, "I am the <u>way</u> *road* and the truth and *Jesus.*
the life. No one comes to the Father except through me."

Ephesians 2:13: In Christ Jesus you who once were far away
have been <u>brought near</u> through the blood of Christ.

Ephesians 3:12: In him and <u>through faith</u> in him we may
approach God with freedom and confidence.
boldness   confident access

Hebrews 4:16: Let us then approach the throne of grace with
confidence, so that we may <u>receive mercy</u> and <u>find grace</u> to
<u>help us</u> in our time of need.

Hebrews 7:25: He is able to save completely those who come to God through him, because he always lives to intercede for them.

Hebrews 10:22: Let us draw near to God with a sincere heart in full assurance of faith, having our hearts sprinkled to cleanse us from a guilty conscience and having our bodies washed with pure water.

James 4:8: Come near to God and he will come near to you.

Confession

Lord, I have not taken full advantage of the access that you have given me to you. Please forgive me for not praying often enough, for not looking to you for everything, for not even wanting to come to you when you have made yourself available every moment of the day. I have been negligent and am truly sorry and repent.

Thanksgiving

Thank you for being accessible.
Thank you that you are near whenever I pray (Deut. 4:7).
Thank you that the one thing I should seek is to be close to you, to gaze at your beauty, to worship you, and to fellowship with you (Ps. 27:4).
Thank you that when I go in my room and close the door and pray, you will reward me (Matt. 6:6).
Thank you that I know that Jesus is the way, the truth, and the life, and that I can come to you through him (John 14:6).
Thank you that although I was once far away, now I have

been brought near to you through the blood of Christ (Eph. 2:13).

Thank you that in Christ and through faith in him I can approach you with freedom and confidence (Eph. 3:12).

Thank you that I can approach you with confidence and receive mercy and find grace to help me in my need (Heb. 4:16).

Thank you that you save me completely because Jesus intercedes for me (Heb. 7:25).

Thank you that I can draw near to you when my heart is sincere and I come in faith (Heb. 10:22).

Thank you that when I come near to you, you will come near to me (James 4:8).

Supplication

Deut 4:7 how to be near — call.
whenever I call! I get so used to going
on feelings & sights. By faith I can
access this INCREDIBLE truth.

Psalm 27:4
David wanted to be near God — not for
favors, but just because He is the
most beautiful & delightful of
all things created or known.
(what it is like to be near)

Matt. 6:6
singular & private
unseen.

Supplication

Thank you that when I look to you,
you are always looking at me.

Thank you that when I'm feeling
un·noticed, I can remember
that you are the Great Noticer

not only do you notice
but you *know*

2

CREATOR

Adoration

Genesis 1:1: <u>In the beginning God</u> created the heavens and the earth.

Genesis 1:3: And God <u>said</u>, "Let there be light," and there was light.

Psalm 19:1: The heavens declare the glory of God; the skies proclaim the work of his hands.

Psalm 121:2: My help comes from the LORD, <u>the Maker of</u> heaven and earth.

Isaiah 51:16: I have put my words in your mouth and covered you with the shadow of my hand—I who set the heavens in place, who laid the foundations of the earth, and who say to Zion, "You are my people."

Isaiah 66:2: "Has not my hand made all these things, and so they came into being?" declares the LORD. "This is the one I esteem: he who is humble and contrite in spirit, and trembles at my word."

Jeremiah 27:5: With my great power and outstretched arm I made the earth and its people and the animals that are on it, and I give it to anyone I please.

Jeremiah 32:17: Ah, Sovereign LORD, you have made the heavens and the earth by your great power and outstretched arm. Nothing is too hard for you.

2 Corinthians 5:5: God . . . has made us [to be clothed with our heavenly dwelling] and has given us the Spirit as a deposit, guaranteeing what is to come.

Hebrews 3:4: Every house is built by someone, but <u>God is the builder of everything.</u>

Confession

I at times fail to worship you as the Creator of everything that is. In spite of the evidence in the heavens and on earth, I often forget that you made it all. Forgive me for not trusting you in the little things when you are able to do anything you will to do. And forgive me for not thanking you for creating me just the way you did.

Thanksgiving

Thank you for creating the world and for creating me.
Thank you that there was a beginning; I did not just evolve (Gen. 1:1).
Thank you that when you say, "Let there be light" there will be light in any situation (Gen. 1:3).
Thank you that the heavens declare your glory and the skies proclaim your creativity (Ps. 19:1).
Thank you that my help comes from you and from no place else (Ps. 121:2).
Thank you that you set the heavens in place and laid the foundations of the earth, and that you can certainly

put words in my mouth and keep your hand on me
(Isa. 51:16).

Thank you that your hand made everything, that you
esteem me when I am humble and teachable in spirit
and tremble at your words to me (Isa. 66:2).

Thank you that not only did you create the earth and
everything and everybody on it but you have the right
to give it to anyone you please (Jer. 27:5).

Thank you that you are sovereign and have such power
that nothing is too hard for you (Jer. 32:17).

Thank you that you made me for a purpose and guaran-
teed it by giving me the Holy Spirit as a deposit of
what is to come (2 Cor. 5:5).

Thank you that you are the builder of everything, and that
you use me as a tool (Heb. 3:4).

Supplication

Supplication

3

ETERNAL

Adoration

Deuteronomy 33:27: The eternal God is your refuge, and underneath are the everlasting arms. He will drive out your enemy before you.

Psalm 90:1: Lord, you have been our dwelling place throughout all generations.

Psalm 90:2: Before the mountains were born or you brought forth the earth and the world, from everlasting to everlasting you are God.

Psalm 102:27: You remain the same, and your years will never end.

Isaiah 40:28: The LORD is the everlasting God, the Creator of the ends of the earth. He will not grow tired or weary, and his understanding no one can fathom.

Isaiah 46:4: Even to your old age and gray hairs I am he, I am he who will sustain you. I have made you and I will carry you; I will sustain you and I will rescue you.

Hebrews 9:14: How much more, then, will the blood of Christ, who through the eternal Spirit offered himself unblemished to God, cleanse our consciences from acts that lead to death, so that we may serve the living God!

2 Peter 3:8: With the Lord a day is like a thousand years, and a thousand years are like a day.

Revelation 4:8: Holy, holy, holy is the Lord God Almighty, who was, and is, and is to come.

Revelation 4:9: The living creatures give glory, honor and thanks to him who sits on the throne and who lives for ever and ever.

Revelation 16:5: You are just in these judgments, you who are and who were, the Holy One, because you have so judged.

Confession

Forgive me, Lord, for sometimes forgetting that you are eternal and for not thanking you for your eternal love for me. I also waste much time on things that are not of eternal value. Cleanse my life of such things, reminding me that I will live with you forever. Therefore, it matters what I do now. I must use these days in preparation for eternity.

Thanksgiving

Thank you for being eternal and for giving me eternal life
 with you.
Thank you that you are my refuge and that your arms
 underneath me are everlasting (Deut. 33:27).

Thank you that you have always been my dwelling place
and that you always will be (Ps. 90:1).

Thank you that, because you were before everything, you
created everything (Ps. 90:2).

Thank you that you will always remain the same
(Ps. 102:27).

Thank you that you will never grow tired or weary
(Isa. 40:28).

Thank you that even into my old age you will sustain me.
You have made me, and you will carry me through
(Isa. 46:4).

Thank you that the blood of Christ through the eternal
Spirit will cleanse my conscience so that I may serve
you (Heb. 9:14).

Thank you that I can't put you on my timetable. You are
outside of time and you put me on your timetable
(2 Peter 3:8).

Thank you that all creatures, including me, will spend
eternity praising you and giving you glory, honor, and
thanks (Rev. 4:8–9).

Thank you that you are just in your judgments now
because you were always just (Rev. 16:5).

Supplication

Supplication

4

FAITHFUL

Adoration

Genesis 28:15: I am with you and will watch over you wherever you go, and I will bring you back to this land. I will not leave you until I have done what I have promised you.

Joshua 23:14: Now I am about to go the way of all the earth. You know with all your heart and soul that not one of all the good promises the LORD your God gave you has failed. Every promise has been fulfilled; not one has failed.

2 Timothy 2:19: God's solid foundation stands firm, sealed with this inscription: "The Lord knows those who are his," and, "Everyone who confesses the name of the Lord must turn away from wickedness."

Titus 1:2: Faith and knowledge rest[s] on the hope of eternal life, which God, who does not lie, promised before the beginning of time.

Hebrews 6:10: God is not unjust; he will not forget your work and the love you have shown him as you have helped his people and continue to help them.

Hebrews 10:22: Let us draw near to God with a sincere heart in full assurance of faith, having our hearts sprinkled to cleanse us from a guilty conscience and having our bodies washed with pure water.

Hebrews 10:23: Let us hold unswervingly to the hope we profess, for he who promised is faithful.

1 Peter 4:19: Those who suffer according to God's will should commit themselves to their faithful Creator and continue to do good.

2 Peter 3:9: The Lord is not slow in keeping his promise, as some understand slowness. He is patient with you, not wanting anyone to perish, but everyone to come to repentance.

1 John 1:9: If we confess our sins, he is faithful and just and will forgive us our sins and purify us from all unrighteousness.

Revelation 6:10: They called out in a loud voice, "How long, Sovereign Lord, holy and true, until you judge the inhabitants of the earth and avenge our blood?"

Confession

O Lord, you have always been faithful to me, but I have not always been faithful to you. I have not always trusted you to be faithful even though you have proved yourself to me again and again. Please forgive me for my lack of trust in who you are and what you can and will do.

Thanksgiving

Thank you that, because you are a faithful God, I can
believe everything you have written in the Scriptures.

Thank you that you are with me and watch over me
wherever I go. You won't leave me until you have done
all you have promised (Gen. 28:15).

Thank you that not one of all the good promises you give
me will fail. Every promise will be fulfilled (Josh.
23:14).

Thank you that you know those who are yours and
therefore you know me (2 Tim. 2:19).

Thank you that there is eternal life; you do not lie and
you promised it before the beginning of time
(Titus 1:2).

Thank you that you won't forget my work and my love for
you that I've shown by helping others (Heb. 6:10).

Thank you that I can draw near to you in full assurance
that I have what you have promised (Heb. 10:22–23).

Thank you that when I suffer according to your will it is
possible to commit myself to you as my faithful
Creator and continue to do good (1 Peter 4:19).

Thank you that you are patient with me because you want
everyone to repent (2 Peter 3:9).

Thank you that as soon as I confess my sins they are
forgiven and I am cleansed from all unrighteousness
(1 John 1:9).

Thank you that some day you will judge the inhabitants
of the earth and avenge the blood of your people
(Rev. 6:10).

Supplication

Supplication

5

FATHER

Matthew 5:44–45: Love your enemies and pray for those who persecute you, that you may be sons of your Father in heaven. He causes his sun to rise on the evil and the good, and sends rain on the righteous and the unrighteous.

Matthew 10:20: It will not be you speaking, but the Spirit of your Father speaking through you.

Matthew 18:19: If two of you on earth agree about anything you ask for, it will be done for you by my Father in heaven.

Matthew 26:39: My Father, if it is possible, may this cup be taken from me. Yet not as I will, but as you will.

Luke 11:13: If you then, though you are evil, know how to give good gifts to your children, how much more will your Father in heaven give the Holy Spirit to those who ask him!

John 6:27: Do not work for food that spoils, but for food that endures to eternal life, which the Son of Man will give you. On him God the Father has placed his seal of approval.

John 14:13: I will do whatever you ask in my name, so that the Son may bring glory to the Father.

John 14:26: The Counselor, the Holy Spirit, whom the Father will send in my name, will teach you all things and will remind you of everything I have said to you.

1 John 2:1: My dear children, I write this to you so that you will not sin. But if anybody does sin, we have one who speaks to the Father in our defense—Jesus Christ, the Righteous One.

Jude 1: To those who have been called, who are loved by God the Father and kept by Jesus Christ.

Confession

Dear Father, I have not loved you as my Father every moment. I have not always recognized nor thanked you for all that you have done for me as a loving Father. Neither have I always been a good parent to my own children. Please forgive me and cause me to come frequently to you for your loving care, and then extend that care to my family.

Thanksgiving

Thank you for being my Father.
Thank you that as your child I must love my enemies and
    pray for those who persecute me (Matt. 5:44–45).
Thank you that you will speak through me; I won't have
    to do it myself (Matt. 10:20).
Thank you that if two of us agree about something and
    ask you for it, if it is within your will, it will be done
    for us (Matt. 18:19).

Thank you that if it is possible you will take away my
 suffering. If not, it is your will for me (Matt. 26:39).
Thank you that you will give me the Holy Spirit when I
 ask you (Luke 11:13).
Thank you that as your child I do not need to work for
 food that spoils because you will take care of my
 needs. Food that spoils can mean being fed by the
 approval and praise of men, but I can concentrate on
 the things that are eternal. Those are the things that
 Jesus gives me to do, and what Jesus gives me will be
 approved by you (John 6:27).
Thank you that, if it is within your will, you will do
 whatever I ask in Jesus' name, so that through me Jesus
 will bring glory to you (John 14:13).
Thank you that you have sent me the Holy Spirit who will
 teach me all things and will remind me of everything
 Jesus has said (John 14:26).
Thank you that if I sin, you give me Jesus to speak to you
 in my defense (1 John 2:1).
Thank you that as one called by you, I am loved by you as
 my Father and kept by Jesus Christ (Jude 1).

Supplication

Supplication

6

GLORY

1 Kings 19:12: After the earthquake came a fire, but the LORD was not in the fire. And after the fire came a gentle whisper.

Psalm 19:1: The heavens declare the glory of God; the skies proclaim the work of his hands.

Psalm 46:10: Be still, and know that I am God; I will be exalted among the nations, I will be exalted in the earth.

Isaiah 55:9: As the heavens are higher than the earth, so are my ways higher than your ways and my thoughts than your thoughts.

John 14:13: I will do whatever you ask in my name, so that the Son may bring glory to the Father.

2 Corinthians 1:20: No matter how many promises God has made, they are "Yes" in Christ. And so through him the "Amen" is spoken by us to the glory of God.

2 Corinthians 4:15: All this is for your benefit, so that the grace that is reaching more and more people may cause thanksgiving to overflow to the glory of God.

Philippians 1:11: [May you be] filled with the fruit of righteousness that comes through Jesus Christ—to the glory and praise of God.

Philippians 4:19: God will meet all your needs according to his glorious riches in Christ Jesus.

Revelation 15:8: The temple was filled with smoke from the glory of God and from his power, and no one could enter the temple until the seven plagues of the seven angels were completed.

Confession

Too often I forget that my life is to be lived for your glory, and I take the glory for something rather than give it to you. Neither have I always glorified you with my witness and words. Forgive me for thinking too much of myself and too little of your magnificent glory.

Thanksgiving

Thank you that someday I will see your glory face to face.
Thank you that your glory often comes as a gentle whisper (1 Kings 19:12).
Thank you that the heavens declare your glory and the skies tell of the work of your hands. I can always look up and see your glory (Ps. 19:1).
Thank you that I can be still and will know that you are God, and that you will be exalted among the nations (Ps. 46:10).

Thank you that your ways are higher than my ways and that your thoughts are higher—much higher—than my thoughts (Isa. 55:9).

Thank you that, if it be within your will, Jesus will do whatever I ask in his name so that he may bring glory to you (John 14:13).

Thank you that no matter how many promises you have made, they are all "yes," that is, your promises are kept in Christ, and my believing them will bring glory to you (2 Cor. 1:20).

Thank you that my every situation is designed for my benefit, so that the grace you have given me might flow through me to others, causing them to thank you and bring glory to you (2 Cor. 4:15).

Thank you that I am filled with the fruit of righteousness because this brings glory to you. This righteousness is in Jesus Christ (Phil. 1:11).

Thank you for meeting all my needs according to your glorious riches in Christ Jesus (Phil. 4:19).

Thank you that your glory will be visible throughout eternity (Rev. 15:8).

Supplication

Supplication

7

GOOD

Adoration

Psalm 25:8: Good and upright is the LORD; therefore he instructs sinners in his ways.

Psalm 33:5: The LORD loves righteousness and justice; the earth is full of his unfailing love.

Psalm 34:8: Taste and see that the LORD is good; blessed is the man who takes refuge in him.

Psalm 68:19: Praise be to the Lord, to God our Savior, who daily bears our burdens.

Psalm 107:9: He satisfies the thirsty and fills the hungry with good things.

Lamentations 3:25: The LORD is good to those whose hope is in him, to the one who seeks him.

Matthew 7:11: If you, then, though you are evil, know how to give good gifts to your children, how much more will your Father in heaven give good gifts to those who ask him!

Luke 6:35: But love your enemies, do good to them, and lend to them without expecting to get anything back. Then your reward will be great, and you will be sons of the Most High, because he is kind to the ungrateful and wicked.

Romans 2:4: Do you show contempt for the riches of his kindness, tolerance and patience, not realizing that God's kindness leads you toward repentance?

Titus 3:4: But when the kindness and love of God our Savior appeared, he saved us.

Confession

Dear Lord, because you are good you give good gifts. You have satisfied me with so many good things, and I often fail to acknowledge them or give thanks to you. Forgive my ingratitude and my presumption upon your grace to me. Often I have doubted your good will. I think of you as a prohibitive God instead of a good and gracious God. Please forgive me.

Thanksgiving

Thank you, Lord, for being so good to me.
Thank you that you are also upright and that you guide me in your ways (Ps. 25:8).
Thank you that you love righteousness and justice and that the earth is full of your unfailing love (Ps. 33:5).
Thank you that, because you are good to the taste, when I think about you, you satisfy me. Thank you that I will be happiest when I continue to read the Bible to see what you say, and when I let you surround me and protect me with your love (Ps. 34:8).

Thank you that every day you bear my burdens
(Ps. 68:19).
Thank you that you satisfy me when I am thirsty, and that
when I am hungry you fill me with good things
(Ps. 107:9).
Thank you that you are good to me when my hope is in
you and when I seek you out (Lam. 3:25).
Thank you that whenever I want a good gift, I can come
to you as my Father in heaven and you will give to me
far better gifts than any earthly father would (Matt.
7:11).
Thank you that I am to love and do good to my enemies,
not expecting anything in return. You are kind to the
ungrateful, and I should be like you (Luke 6:35).
Thank you that your kindness leads to repentance
(Rom. 2:4).
Thank you that you will show me your kindness and love
every day, even today (Titus 3:4).

Supplication

Supplication

8

GRACIOUS

Adoration

Exodus 33:17: I will do the very thing you have asked, because I am pleased with you and I know you by name.

Joshua 1:9: Be strong and courageous. Do not be terrified; do not be discouraged, for the LORD your God will be with you wherever you go.

2 Chronicles 15:2: The LORD is with you when you are with him. If you seek him, he will be found by you, but if you forsake him, he will forsake you.

Psalm 84:11: For the LORD God is a sun and shield; the LORD bestows favor and honor; no good thing does he withhold from those whose walk is blameless.

Lamentations 3:24: The LORD is my portion; therefore I will wait for him.

John 15:15: I no longer call you servants, because a servant does not know his master's business. Instead, I have called you friends, for everything that I learned from my Father I have made known to you.

2 Corinthians 4:15: All this is for your benefit, so that the grace that is reaching more and more people may cause thanksgiving to overflow to the glory of God.

2 Corinthians 10:18: It is not the one who commends himself who is approved, but the one whom the Lord commends.

1 Peter 2:9: You are a chosen people, a royal priesthood, a holy nation, a people belonging to God, that you may declare the praises of him who called you out of darkness into his wonderful light.

1 John 4:18: There is no fear in love. But perfect love drives out fear, because fear has to do with punishment. The one who fears is not made perfect in love.

Confession

O God, you are so gracious and I don't always recognize it. Forgive me when I am so self-centered that I don't appreciate that everything comes from your grace. I have done nothing worthwhile on my own; everything is from you. I have not always acknowledged that, and even when I do, I want to think that I deserve a little of it. Please forgive me.

Thanksgiving

Thank you for being so gracious.
Thank you that you are pleased with me because of Jesus, that you know my name and do the very thing I ask of you (Exod. 33:17).
Thank you that when you command me to do something,

I can be strong and courageous and not be afraid or discouraged about doing it, because you will be with me wherever I go (Josh. 1:9).

Thank you that when I want to be with you, you want to be with me. When I go looking for you, you will let me find you; but when I reject you, you won't force your way on me (2 Chron. 15:2).

Thank you that you will withhold no good thing from me when my walk is blameless (Ps. 84:11).

Thank you that you are enough for me. If I wait for you, you will fulfill me. You are my portion (Lam. 3:24).

Thank you that Jesus calls me his friend (John 15:15).

Thank you that whatever happens to me is for my benefit, so that your grace may reach more and more people causing thanksgiving to your glory (2 Cor. 4:15).

Thank you that I am approved by your commendation, not by my own commendation (2 Cor. 10:18).

Thank you that I am chosen by you to praise you, who called me out of darkness into your wonderful light (1 Peter 2:9).

Thank you that when I am sure I am loved, I will no longer be afraid (1 John 4:18).

Supplication

Supplication

9

GUIDE

Adoration

Numbers 10:33: They set out from the mountain of the Lord and traveled for three days. The ark of the covenant of the Lord went before them during those three days to find them a place to rest.

2 Samuel 22:29: You are my lamp, O Lord; the Lord turns my darkness into light.

Psalm 23:2–3: He makes me lie down in green pastures, he leads me beside quiet waters, he restores my soul. He guides me in paths of righteousness for his name's sake.

Psalm 25:5: Guide me in your truth and teach me, for you are God my Savior, and my hope is in you all day long.

Psalm 25:9: He guides the humble in what is right and teaches them his way.

Psalm 31:3: Since you are my rock and my fortress, for the sake of your name lead and guide me.

Psalm 32:8: I will instruct you and teach you in the way you should go; I will counsel you and watch over you.

Luke 1:79: [Jesus came to] shine on those living in darkness and in the shadow of death, to guide our feet into the path of peace.

John 10:3: The watchman opens the gate for him, and the sheep listen to his voice. He calls his own sheep by name and leads them out.

John 16:13: When he, the Spirit of truth, comes, he will guide you into all truth. He will not speak on his own; he will speak only what he hears, and he will tell you what is yet to come.

Confession

I sometimes go my own way, even though I know that you are the perfect guide. Forgive me, Lord, for not looking to you for guidance in every area of my life. It is wrong and just plain stupid not to ask your guidance when you so graciously make it available. I repent and trust your Holy Spirit to prompt me to pray for guidance every day.

Thanksgiving

Thank you for being my guide for all of my life.
Thank you that you will always go before me to find for me a place of rest (Num. 10:33).
Thank you that you are my lamp, who turns my darkness into light (2 Sam. 22:29).
Thank you that you lead me to the place that is quiet, where my soul will be restored—the place of righteousness (Ps. 23:2–3).

Thank you that you will guide me in truth and teach me, because you are God my Savior, so my hope will be in you all day long (Ps. 25:5).

Thank you that when I am humble, you will guide me into what is right and teach me your ways (Ps. 25:9).

Thank you that you will lead me for the sake of your name, since my trust is in you (Ps. 31:3).

Thank you that you will instruct me and teach me in the way I should go; you will counsel me and watch over me (Ps. 32:8).

Thank you that when I am living in the darkness of my own choice, you give me light to guide my feet into the path of peace (Luke 1:79).

Thank you that Jesus, as my Shepherd, calls me by name and leads me where I should go (John 10:3).

Thank you that you have given me the Holy Spirit to guide me into all truth (John 16:13).

Supplication

Supplication

10

HOLY

Adoration

Leviticus 19:2: Speak to the entire assembly of Israel and say to them: "Be holy because I, the LORD your God, am holy."

Deuteronomy 32:4: He is the Rock, his works are perfect, and all his ways are just. A faithful God who does no wrong, upright and just is he.

Psalm 33:4–5: The word of the LORD is right and true; he is faithful in all he does. The LORD loves righteousness and justice; the earth is full of his unfailing love.

Psalm 92:15: The LORD is upright; he is my Rock, and there is no wickedness in him.

Proverbs 9:10: The fear of the LORD is the beginning of wisdom, and knowledge of the Holy One is understanding.

Matthew 5:48: Be perfect, therefore, as your heavenly Father is perfect.

John 17:11: I [Jesus] will remain in the world no longer, but they are still in the world, and I am coming to you. Holy Father, protect them by the power of your name—the name you gave me—so that they may be one as we are one.

James 1:13: When tempted, no one should say, "God is tempting me." For God cannot be tempted by evil, nor does he tempt anyone.

1 John 1:5: This is the message we have heard from him and declare to you: God is light; in him there is no darkness at all.

1 John 2:20: You have an anointing from the Holy One, and all of you know the truth.

Confession

Lord, I confess that I am anything but holy. Forgive me when I have not sought holiness through the power of your Holy Spirit. You command me to be holy because you are holy, and that command is good for me—I want to be like you. You have said that knowledge of you as holy is true understanding, so please help me to know you better as the Holy One.

Thanksgiving

Thank you for being holy.
Thank you that I am commanded to be holy (Lev. 19:2).
Thank you that your works are perfect, all your ways are just, and you do no wrong (Deut. 32:4).
Thank you that your word is right and true. You are faithful in all that you do, and you love righteousness and justice (Ps. 33:4–5).
Thank you that you are my Rock. I can stand on you when I am tempted, because there is no wickedness in

you. You are upright in every way and you are making me like yourself (Ps. 92:15).

Thank you that knowledge of you is understanding (Prov. 9:10).

Thank you that I am to be perfect just as you, as my heavenly Father, are perfect (Matt. 5:48).

Thank you that as my holy Father you will protect me by your holy name so that I may be one with other Christians (John 17:11).

Thank you that you test me to show me what I am, but you never tempt me in order to destroy me (James 1:13).

Thank you that you are light and in you there is no darkness at all. Closeness to you keeps me in the light (1 John 1:5).

Thank you that when I have an anointing from the Holy Spirit I know the truth. The Holy Spirit tells me only truth (1 John 2:20).

Supplication

Supplication

11

IMPARTIAL

Deuteronomy 10:17: The LORD your God is God of gods and Lord of lords, the great God, mighty and awesome, who shows no partiality and accepts no bribes.

Job 36:5: God is mighty, but does not despise men; he is mighty, and firm in his purpose.

Job 37:24: Therefore, men revere him, for does he not have regard for all the wise in heart?

Acts 10:34–35: I now realize how true it is that God does not show favoritism but accepts men from every nation who fear him and do what is right.

Romans 2:6: God "will give to each person according to what he has done."

Romans 2:11: For God does not show favoritism.

Galatians 2:6: As for those who seemed to be important— whatever they were makes no difference to me; God does not judge by external appearance—those men added nothing to my message.

Ephesians 6:8: The Lord will reward everyone for whatever good he does, whether he is slave or free.

Colossians 3:25: Anyone who does wrong will be repaid for his wrong, and there is no favoritism.

1 Peter 1:17: Since you call on a Father who judges each man's work impartially, live your lives as strangers here in reverent fear.

Confession

Your ways are not my ways—how true that is in regard to impartiality. I confess that I am frequently partial to those who do things for me or to those whom I like better than others. You are not partial to anyone. At times I've wanted to make you partial to me, but trying to do so is wrong; you love all people and need no one to do anything for you. Please forgive me and help me to look at others from your viewpoint.

Thanksgiving

Thank you that you are impartial.
Thank you that I cannot bribe you (Deut. 10:17).
Thank you that although you are mighty and firm in your purpose, you do not despise people (Job 36:5).
Thank you that you have regard for those who are wise in heart. You listen to those whose hearts are pure toward you (Job 37:24).
Thank you that you do not show favoritism but accept those from any nation who reverence you and do right (Acts 10:34–35).

Thank you that you give to each person according to what he or she has done—not just what he or she has professed (Rom. 2:6).

Thank you that you will never show favoritism to me or to anyone else (Rom. 2:11).

Thank you that what others are shouldn't make any difference to me because you do not judge by outward appearances and neither should I (Gal. 2:6).

Thank you that you reward everyone—regardless of position—for the good that he or she has done (Eph. 6:8).

Thank you that anyone who does wrong will be repaid for his wrong (Col. 3:25).

Thank you that I should live my life as a stranger here in reverent fear of you, knowing that some day I must give an account for all I have done (1 Peter 1:17).

Supplication

Supplication

12

IMMUTABLE

Adoration

Numbers 23:19: God is not a man, that he should lie, nor a son of man, that he should change his mind. Does he speak and then not act? Does he promise and not fulfill?

Numbers 23:20: I have received a command to bless; [God] has blessed, and I cannot change it.

1 Samuel 15:29: He who is the Glory of Israel does not lie or change his mind; for he is not a man, that he should change his mind.

Job 23:13: [God] stands alone, and who can oppose him? He does whatever he pleases.

Psalm 33:11: The plans of the LORD stand firm forever, the purposes of his heart through all generations.

Proverbs 19:21: Many are the plans in a man's heart, but it is the LORD's purpose that prevails.

Isaiah 40:28: Do you not know? Have you not heard? The LORD is the everlasting God, the Creator of the ends of the earth. He will not grow tired or weary, and his understanding no one can fathom.

Romans 11:29: God's gifts and his call are irrevocable.

Hebrews 6:17: Because God wanted to make the unchanging nature of his purpose very clear to the heirs of what was promised, he confirmed it with an oath.

Hebrews 6:18: God [swore by himself] so that, by two unchangeable things in which it is impossible for God to lie, we who have fled to take hold of the hope offered to us may be greatly encouraged.

James 1:17: Every good and perfect gift is from above, coming down from the Father of the heavenly lights, who does not change like shifting shadows.

Confession

Lord, I confess that at times I don't want you to be immutable. I want you to change your laws so that I can do what I want without being guilty of sin. I'm foolish enough to think that if I wait long enough you might change something. Please forgive me for not thanking you enough that you do not change and for the security that your immutability gives to me and to this world.

Thanksgiving

Thank you for being immutable, for never changing, and for the security it gives me.

Thank you that you will not promise without fulfilling that promise (Num. 23:19).

Thank you that when you decide to bless, I cannot change it (Num. 23:20).

Thank you that you do not lie or change your mind
(1 Sam. 15:29).

Thank you that you stand alone. No one can oppose you
because you do whatever you please (Job 23:13).

Thank you that your plans stand firm forever; nothing can
change them (Ps. 33:11).

Thank you that I may have many plans, but your purpose
will prevail (Prov. 19:21).

Thank you that you are everlasting, that you never change,
and that you never grow tired or weary. You are always
there for me (Isa. 40:28).

Thank you that the gifts you have given to me—to en-
courage and motivate others to love and serve you—
and your call to me to use these gifts have not been
revoked. You want me to use my gifts more and more
(Rom. 11:29).

Thank you that the very nature of your purpose is unchanging. You have made that clear so that I will be encouraged—especially when I realize that your purpose is to
conform me to your image (Heb. 6:17–18).

Thank you that every good and perfect gift is from you.
Because you don't change like shifting shadows, you
have always given good gifts and you always will
(James 1:17).

Supplication

Supplication

13

INCOMPREHENSIBLE

Adoration

Deuteronomy 29:29: The secret things belong to the LORD our God, but the things revealed belong to us and to our children forever, that we may follow all the words of this law.

Job 5:8: If it were I, I would appeal to God; I would lay my cause before him.

Job 5:9: He performs wonders that cannot be fathomed, miracles that cannot be counted.

Job 26:14: And these are but the outer fringe of his works; how faint the whisper we hear of him! Who then can understand the thunder of his power?

Ecclesiastes 3:11: He has made everything beautiful in its time. He has also set eternity in the hearts of men; yet they cannot fathom what God has done from beginning to end.

Isaiah 40:28: Do you not know? Have you not heard? The LORD is the everlasting God, the Creator of the ends of the earth. He will not grow tired or weary, and his understanding no one can fathom.

Isaiah 55:8: "For my thoughts are not your thoughts, neither are your ways my ways," declares the LORD.

Matthew 11:27: All things have been committed to me by my Father. No one knows the Son except the Father, and no one knows the Father except the Son and those to whom the Son chooses to reveal him.

Romans 11:33: Oh, the depth of the riches of the wisdom and knowledge of God! How unsearchable his judgments, and his paths beyond tracing out!

Romans 11:34: Who has known the mind of the Lord? Or who has been his counselor?

1 Corinthians 2:11: Who among men knows the thoughts of a man except the man's spirit within him? In the same way no one knows the thoughts of God except the Spirit of God.

1 Corinthians 2:16: Who has known the mind of the Lord that he may instruct him? But we have the mind of Christ.

Confession

Lord, at times I try to find you outside of Jesus Christ. Forgive me for attempting to know you by looking within instead of trusting you to reveal yourself to me through Christ in the Scriptures.

Thanksgiving

Thank you for revealing to me as much of yourself as you know I can grasp.

Thank you that although the secret things belong to you, the things you have revealed belong to me and my children so that we may obey you (Deut. 29:29).

Thank you that I can appeal to you and lay my cause before you, because you perform wonders that cannot be fathomed and miracles that cannot be counted (Job 5:8–9).

Thank you that if I can hardly understand the quiet beauty of dawn, how could I possibly understand the thunder of your mighty power? (Job 26:14).

Thank you that you have made everything beautiful even though I cannot fathom it (Eccl. 3:11).

Thank you that as the everlasting God and Creator of the ends of the earth, you will not grow tired or weary, and that I cannot fathom the depths of your understanding of all things, including me (Isa. 40:28).

Thank you that your thoughts are not my thoughts and your ways are not my ways (Isa. 55:8).

Thank you that only Jesus really knows you. I cannot know you unless Jesus chooses to reveal you to me (Matt. 11:27).

Thank you that I can never know the depth of your wisdom and knowledge. Your judgments and your paths are beyond me. I will never fully know your mind or be able to advise you. All I can do is believe and obey you, and that is enough (Rom. 11:33–34).

Thank you that no one knows your thoughts except the Holy Spirit. If I want to know your thoughts, I must ask the Holy Spirit (1 Cor. 2:11).

Thank you that I cannot know your mind except through the mind of Christ, which you have revealed to me (1 Cor. 2:16).

Supplication

Supplication

14

INFINITE

Adoration

Exodus 3:14: God said to Moses, "I AM WHO I AM. This is what you are to say to the Israelites: 'I AM has sent me to you.'"

Deuteronomy 32:40: I lift my hand to heaven and declare: As surely as I live forever . . .

1 Kings 8:27: Will God really dwell on earth? The heavens, even the highest heaven, cannot contain you. How much less this temple I have built!

Job 35:6–8: If you sin, how does that affect him? If your sins are many, what does that do to him? If you are righteous, what do you give to him, or what does he receive from your hand? Your wickedness affects only a man like yourself, and your righteousness only the sons of men.

Psalm 147:5: Great is our Lord and mighty in power; his understanding has no limit.

Isaiah 44:6: This is what the LORD says—Israel's King and Redeemer, the LORD Almighty: I am the first and I am the last; apart from me there is no God.

Jeremiah 10:10: The LORD is the true God; he is the living God, the eternal King. When he is angry, the earth trembles; the nations cannot endure his wrath.

Jeremiah 23:24: "Can anyone hide in secret places so that I cannot see him?" declares the LORD. "Do not I fill heaven and earth?" declares the LORD.

John 5:26: As the Father has life in himself, so he has granted the Son to have life in himself.

Acts 17:24–25: The God who made the world and everything in it is the Lord of heaven and earth and does not live in temples built by hands. And he is not served by human hands, as if he needed anything, because he himself gives all men life and breath and everything else.

Confession

Lord, my thoughts about you are too small. I confess that I look at my circumstances without consideration that you are infinite, and that you know, perform, and love without limit. Forgive me for my shortsightedness.

Thanksgiving

Thank you that your love and your power have no limits.
Thank you that you are who you are. Your name is I AM because you need nothing; you are self-existent. You are not dependent upon anyone or anything (Exod. 3:14).
Thank you that you live forever; I know that you do because you declare that you do (Deut. 32:40).

Thank you that the heavens cannot contain you and
neither can anything that I have built—either materi-
ally or in my mind (1 Kings 8:27).

Thank you that my sin and my righteousness do not affect
you, but they do affect me and those around me (Job
35:6–8).

Thank you that your power and understanding have no
limit (Ps. 147:5).

Thank you that you are the first and the last. Apart from
you there is no God (Isa. 44:6).

Thank you that you are the true God. You are living, and
you are my eternal King (Jer. 10:10).

Thank you that you fill heaven and earth. Nothing is too
big for you to take care of, therefore, I can relax (Jer.
23:24).

Thank you that you have life in yourself and you are not
dependent upon anything else (John 5:26).

Thank you that you do not need anything that human
hands can do for you, because you yourself give life
and breath and everything else (Acts 17:24–25).

Supplication

Supplication

15

INVISIBLE

Adoration

Deuteronomy 4:15: You saw no form of any kind the day the LORD spoke to you at Horeb out of the fire. Therefore watch yourselves very carefully.

Deuteronomy 5:22: These are the commandments the LORD proclaimed in a loud voice to your whole assembly there on the mountain from out of the fire, the cloud and the deep darkness; and he added nothing more. Then he wrote them on two stone tablets and gave them to me.

Job 9:11: When he passes me, I cannot see him; when he goes by, I cannot perceive him.

Psalm 97:2: Clouds and thick darkness surround him; righteousness and justice are the foundation of his throne.

John 1:18: No one has ever seen God, but God the One and Only, who is at the Father's side, has made him known.

John 6:46: No one has seen the Father except the one who is from God; only he has seen the Father.

Romans 1:20: For since the creation of the world God's invisible qualities—his eternal power and divine nature—

have been clearly seen, being understood from what has been made, so that men are without excuse.

Colossians 1:15: He is the image of the invisible God, the firstborn over all creation.

Hebrews 11:27: By faith he left Egypt, not fearing the king's anger; he persevered because he saw him who is invisible.

1 John 4:12: No one has ever seen God; but if we love one another, God lives in us and his love is made complete in us.

Confession

Forgive me, Lord, for doubting your presence just because I cannot see you. I too often do what I want, not considering you, because you are invisible to my human eyes. I have not even appreciated that you are apparent in creation and, especially, in your written Word. I repent and will look for you in everything.

Thanksgiving

Thank you that I must exercise faith in order to see you.
Thank you that you do not show me your form but you
    let me hear your voice (Deut. 4:15).
Thank you that sometimes you speak to me out of the
    fire—that judgment you make on my actions and
    words—and I know it is you even though I cannot see
    you (Deut. 5:22).

Thank you that when you pass me, I cannot see you;
   when you go by, I cannot perceive you, but that
   doesn't mean that you are not there (Job 9:11).
Thank you that, even though you conceal yourself from
   my eyesight, you rule with righteousness and justice.
   Thus, I can trust you (Ps. 97:2).
Thank you that no one has ever seen you, but that Jesus
   shows you to me (John 1:18).
Thank you that no one has seen you, Father, except Jesus
   Christ who was with you from the beginning (John
   6:46).
Thank you that I am still without excuse when I sin,
   because you have made your invisible qualities to be
   seen clearly in your power and your divine nature
   (Rom. 1:20).
Thank you that, although I cannot see you, Christ is the
   exact image of you and the firstborn of all who will
   someday be conformed to your image (Col. 1:15).
Thank you that I can persevere when I see you by faith,
   even though you are invisible to my eyes (Heb. 11:27).
Thank you that although I cannot see you, I know that
   you are alive, because you live in others. You
   demonstrate your life in me and others as we love each
   other (1 John 4:12).

Supplication

Supplication

16

JEALOUS

Adoration

Exodus 20:5: You shall not bow down to them or worship them; for I, the LORD your God, am a jealous God, punishing the children for the sin of the fathers to the third and fourth generation of those who hate me.

Exodus 20:7: You shall not misuse the name of the LORD your God, for the LORD will not hold anyone guiltless who misuses his name.

Exodus 34:14: Do not worship any other god, for the LORD, whose name is Jealous, is a jealous God.

Deuteronomy 4:24: The LORD your God is a consuming fire, a jealous God.

Joshua 24:19: You are not able to serve the LORD. He is a holy God; he is a jealous God. He will not forgive your rebellion and your sins.

2 Chronicles 16:9: The eyes of the LORD range throughout the earth to strengthen those whose hearts are fully committed to him.

Isaiah 30:1–2: "Woe to the obstinate children," declares the LORD, "to those who carry out plans that are not mine, forming an alliance, but not by my Spirit, heaping sin upon sin; who go down to Egypt without consulting me; who look for help to Pharaoh's protection, to Egypt's shade for refuge."

Ezekiel 23:25: I will direct my jealous anger against you, and they will deal with you in fury. They will cut off your noses and your ears, and those of you who are left will fall by the sword. They will take away your sons and daughters, and those of you who are left will be consumed by fire.

Ezekiel 39:25: This is what the Sovereign LORD says: I will now bring Jacob back from captivity and will have compassion on all the people of Israel, and I will be zealous for my holy name.

1 Corinthians 10:22: Are we trying to arouse the Lord's jealousy? Are we stronger than he?

Confession

O Lord, I confess that I am constantly putting things and others before you. I worship idols more than I even realize. I go to others for help when I have you to go to. Moreover, I use your name in ways that I should not. I repent of these sins that I commit again and again, and I will take the help that comes from your Holy Spirit.

Thanksgiving

Thank you for being jealous for my love and worship. Thank you that I am not to bow down and worship any other god (Exod. 20:5).

Thank you for telling me to never misuse your name. And
that doesn't mean just swearing but also calling myself
a Christian and then not acting like one (Exod. 20:7).
Thank you for telling me that I am not to worship any
other god (Exod. 34:14).
Thank you that you are a consuming fire—that you
intend to consume my whole life (Deut. 4:24).
Thank you that you don't let just anybody serve you. You
are holy and are not willing to use people who are
rebellious and sinful, but you are willing to let me
serve you (Josh. 24:19).
Thank you that your eyes look throughout the earth for
those who are fully committed to you so you can
strengthen them (2 Chron. 16:9).
Thank you for telling me that I heap sin upon sin when I
obstinately carry out plans that are not yours, when I
form alliances that are not of your Spirit, when I go for
help without consulting you, when I look in the wrong
place for protection and refuge (Isa. 30:1–2).
Thank you that when you are angry at me, it is because
you are jealous. You want me for your own, and you
do what it takes to make me see that (Ezek. 23:25).
Thank you that you care that your name be kept holy
(Ezek. 39:25).
Thank you for telling me how foolish it would be to
arouse your jealousy. I would certainly know the
consequences, because you are much stronger than I
am (1 Cor. 10:22).

Supplication

Supplication

17

JUST

Adoration

Proverbs 17:3: The crucible for silver and the furnace for gold, but the LORD tests the heart.

Proverbs 21:3: To do what is right and just is more acceptable to the LORD than sacrifice.

Proverbs 24:12: If you say, "But we knew nothing about this," does not he who weighs the heart perceive it? Does not he who guards your life know it? Will he not repay each person according to what he has done?

Isaiah 30:18: The LORD longs to be gracious to you; he rises to show you compassion. For the LORD is a God of justice. Blessed are all who wait for him!

Jeremiah 9:24: "Let him who boasts boast about this: that he understands and knows me, that I am the LORD, who exercises kindness, justice and righteousness on earth, for in these I delight," declares the LORD.

Hebrews 10:30: We know him who said, "It is mine to avenge; I will repay," and again, "The Lord will judge his people."

Hebrews 12:29: Our "God is a consuming fire."

1 Peter 1:17: Since you call on a Father who judges each man's work impartially, live your lives as strangers here in reverent fear.

2 Peter 2:9: The Lord knows how to rescue godly men from trials and to hold the unrighteous for the day of judgment, while continuing their punishment.

1 John 1:9: If we confess our sins, he is faithful and just and will forgive us our sins and purify us from all unrighteousness.

Confession

Lord, I confess that I have at times doubted your justice. So many things seem to be wrong, and I become impatient and discouraged as I look at the world. On the other hand I do not want you to be just with me, because I deserve death. I want you to be merciful to me but just with others. Forgive me for my selfish thinking.

Thanksgiving

Thank you for being just and for Jesus Christ, who bore your just punishment for my sins.

Thank you that you test every heart (Prov. 17:3).

Thank you that my doing what is right and just is more acceptable to you than sacrifice (Prov. 21:3).

Thank you that, whether or not I know what I have done, you know it and you repay me accordingly (Prov. 24:12).

Thank you that even in your justice you long to be gracious to me and to show me compassion. I need to be patient and wait for you to show your loving justice (Isa. 30:18).

Thank you that I can boast in your justice, kindness, and righteousness. The only thing that I, in fact, can boast about is that I understand something of you (Jer. 9:24).

Thank you that it is your right—not mine—to avenge (Heb. 10:30).

Thank you that you are a consuming fire, and that fire is the symbol of judgment (Heb. 12:29).

Thank you that you judge every person's work impartially; therefore I should live my life here as a stranger, not being concerned with the world's values, but having a reverent fear of you (1 Peter 1:17).

Thank you that you know how to rescue me from trials and at the same time hold for judgment those who are not right with you (2 Peter 2:9).

Thank you that if I confess my sins, you are faithful to me. And yet you are just in forgiving my sin because Jesus Christ took the punishment I deserved so that I could be purified from all unrighteousness (1 John 1:9).

Supplication

Supplication

18

LONG-SUFFERING

Adoration

Numbers 14:18: The LORD is slow to anger, abounding in love and forgiving sin and rebellion. Yet he does not leave the guilty unpunished; he punishes the children for the sin of the fathers to the third and fourth generation.

Psalm 86:15: You, O Lord, are a compassionate and gracious God, slow to anger, abounding in love and faithfulness.

Jeremiah 7:23: I gave them this command: Obey me, and I will be your God and you will be my people. Walk in all the ways I command you, that it may go well with you.

Jeremiah 15:15: You understand, O LORD; remember me and care for me. Avenge me on my persecutors. You are long-suffering—do not take me away; think of how I suffer reproach for your sake.

Ezekiel 20:17: I looked on them with pity and did not destroy them or put an end to them in the desert.

Acts 17:30: In the past God overlooked such ignorance, but now he commands all people everywhere to repent.

Romans 2:4: Do you show contempt for the riches of his kindness, tolerance and patience, not realizing that God's kindness leads you toward repentance?

Romans 15:5: May the God who gives endurance and encouragement give you a spirit of unity among yourselves as you follow Christ Jesus.

1 Peter 3:20: [The spirits in prison] disobeyed long ago when God waited patiently in the days of Noah while the ark was being built. In it only a few people, eight in all, were saved through water.

Revelation 2:21–22: I have given [that woman Jezebel] time to repent of her immorality, but she is unwilling. So I will cast her on a bed of suffering, and I will make those who commit adultery with her suffer intensely, unless they repent of her ways.

Confession

O Lord, I have presumed upon your patience. Forgive me for being so slow to repent when you have been so tolerant and kind to me. Through the power of your Spirit, help me to repent quickly and daily for those things that are sinful in my life. Help me, too, to become more kind and patient with others.

Thanksgiving

Thank you for being patient with me.
Thank you that you are slow to anger and abound in love, forgiving my sin and rebellion (Num. 14:18).

Thank you that you are compassionate and gracious, and that you are faithful (Ps. 86:15).

Thank you that I am to obey you because you are my God and I am your child. If I walk in all the ways you command me, it will go well with me (Jer. 7:23).

Thank you that you understand. You remember me and care for me, and you will avenge me (Jer. 15:15).

Thank you that you look on me with pity and do not destroy me or put an end to me (Ezek. 20:17).

Thank you that in the past you overlooked ignorance, but now that people everywhere have your revelation in the Bible, you command us to repent. I am especially accountable because of the knowledge given to me (Acts 17:30).

Thank you that your kindness, tolerance, and patience lead me to repentance (Rom. 2:4).

Thank you that you give endurance and encouragement in answer to prayer, and you will also give a spirit of unity to those who believe (Rom. 15:5).

Thank you that just as you waited patiently in Noah's day, so you wait patiently in our day until the right time for judgment (1 Peter 3:20).

Thank you that you give me time to repent of immorality, but if I don't repent I will suffer intensely (Rev. 2:21–22).

Supplication

Supplication

19

LOVE

Adoration

Deuteronomy 33:12: Let the beloved of the LORD rest secure in him, for he shields him all day long, and the one the LORD loves rests between his shoulders.

Job 7:17: What is man that you make so much of him, that you give him so much attention.

Psalm 63:3: Because your love is better than life, my lips will glorify you.

Psalm 89:33: I will not take my love from him, nor will I ever betray my faithfulness.

Isaiah 38:17: Surely it was for my benefit that I suffered such anguish. In your love you kept me from the pit of destruction; you have put all my sins behind your back.

John 14:21: Whoever has my commands and obeys them, he is the one who loves me. He who loves me will be loved by my Father, and I too will love him and show myself to him.

John 14:23: Jesus replied, "If anyone loves me, he will obey my teaching. My Father will love him, and we will come to him and make our home with him."

Romans 5:8: God demonstrates his own love for us in this: While we were still sinners, Christ died for us.

1 John 4:8: Whoever does not love does not know God, because God is love.

Revelation 14:1: Then I looked, and there before me was the Lamb, standing on Mount Zion, and with him 144,000 who had his name and his Father's name written on their foreheads.

Confession

O Lord, I have so often asked you to show your love to me, even though your love has been revealed in Scripture. Forgive me for not reading the Bible to hear your voice, and for those times when I've read it and not paid attention to it or believed it. I have failed to appreciate that there is no greater expression of love than your giving Jesus to die for me.

Thanksgiving

Thank you for loving me.

Thank you that I can rest secure in you—that you will shield me all day long and I can rest between your shoulders (Deut. 33:12).

Thank you that you give me a lot of attention (Job 7:17).

Thank you that your love is better than life—the experience of your love is so much better than anything life can offer to me without you. Therefore, I should glorify you by telling others about your love (Ps. 63:3).

Thank you that you will not take your love from me, nor

will you ever betray your faithfulness to me (Ps. 89:33).

Thank you that when I am in anguish you use it for my benefit. Your love for me has kept me from the pit of destruction, and you have taken away my sins (Isa. 38:17).

Thank you that when I love the Lord Jesus Christ, he loves me back and shows himself to me. Moreover, I am loved by you (John 14:21).

Thank you that the expression of my love for you is my obedience to you (John 14:23).

Thank you that you demonstrated your love for me by dying for me while I was still a sinner (Rom. 5:8).

Thank you that if I do not love, I do not know you (1 John 4:18).

Thank you that I will be among those who are with Christ in the end because you wrote his name on me (Rev. 14:1).

Supplication

Supplication

20

MERCIFUL

Adoration

2 Samuel 14:14: Like water spilled on the ground, which cannot be recovered, so we must die. But God does not take away life; instead, he devises ways so that a banished person may not remain estranged from him.

Psalm 32:5: I acknowledged my sin to you and did not cover up my iniquity. I said, "I will confess my transgressions to the LORD"—and you forgave the guilt of my sin.

Proverbs 28:13: He who conceals his sins does not prosper, but whoever confesses and renounces them finds mercy.

Jeremiah 29:11: "I know the plans I have for you," declares the LORD, "plans to prosper you and not to harm you, plans to give you hope and a future."

Lamentations 3:32–33: Though he brings grief, he will show compassion, so great is his unfailing love. For he does not willingly bring affliction or grief to the children of men.

2 Corinthians 12:9: [The Lord] said to me, "My grace is sufficient for you, for my power is made perfect in weakness." Therefore I will boast all the more gladly about my weaknesses, so that Christ's power may rest on me.

Hebrews 8:12: I will forgive their wickedness and will remember their sins no more.

James 2:13: Judgment without mercy will be shown to anyone who has not been merciful. Mercy triumphs over judgment!

James 5:15: The prayer offered in faith will make the sick person well; the Lord will raise him up. If he has sinned, he will be forgiven.

1 Peter 5:10: The God of all grace, who called you to his eternal glory in Christ, after you have suffered a little while, will himself restore you and make you strong, firm and steadfast.

Confession

Lord, your mercies are new every morning. But I am so little like you—I show very little mercy to others, while I expect you to show your mercy to me all the time. Please forgive me for my lack of mercy. And forgive me for not being more grateful for the mercy you have extended to me in Jesus Christ.

Thanksgiving

Thank you for your mercy.
Thank you that you devise ways for me to return to you when I have been disobedient (2 Sam. 14:14).
Thank you that when I acknowledge my sin and don't cover it up, but confess it, you forgive the guilt of my sin (Ps. 32:5).

Thank you that when I conceal my sin from you I will not prosper (Prov. 28:13).

Thank you that you have plans for me—not plans to harm, but to prosper me, to give me hope and a future (Jer. 29:11).

Thank you that, although you allow me to feel grief, you also show compassion because you don't willingly bring me affliction or grief. It is all for my good. It's what I need in order to be conformed to your image (Lam. 3:32–33).

Thank you that your grace is always sufficient for me because your power is greater in my weakness (2 Cor. 12:9).

Thank you that you forgive my wickedness and will remember my sins no more (Heb. 8:12).

Thank you for telling me that judgment without mercy will be shown to me when I am not merciful to others (James 2:13).

Thank you that you answer prayer and in your mercy heal those who have sinned (James 5:15).

Thank you that after I have suffered a little while, you will restore me and make me strong, firm, and steadfast (1 Peter 5:10).

Supplication

Supplication

21

OMNIPOTENT

Adoration

Genesis 18:14: Is anything too hard for the LORD?

Numbers 11:23: Is the LORD's arm too short? You will now see whether or not what I say will come true for you.

Job 9:10: He performs wonders that cannot be fathomed, miracles that cannot be counted.

Job 42:2: I know that you can do all things; no plan of yours can be thwarted.

Jeremiah 27:5: [This is what the LORD Almighty says,] "With my great power and outstretched arm I made the earth and its people and the animals that are on it, and I give it to anyone I please."

Matthew 6:13: Lead us not into temptation, but deliver us from the evil one.

Matthew 19:26: Jesus looked at them and said, "With man this is impossible, but with God all things are possible."

Matthew 22:29: Jesus replied, "You are in error because you do not know the Scriptures or the power of God."

Acts 26:8: Why should any of you consider it incredible that God raises the dead?

Revelation 19:1: After this I heard what sounded like the roar of a great multitude in heaven shouting: "Hallelujah! Salvation and glory and power belong to our God."

Confession

Lord, please forgive me for not trusting your power to do anything you desire. So often my conception of you has been too small. I have not asked you to do things that I consider impossible. Please cause me to ask for big things and trust that if they are in your plan that you will do them for your glory.

Thanksgiving

Thank you that you have all power.

Thank you that nothing is too hard for you (Gen. 18:14).

Thank you that your arm is not too short to do anything that you say you will do. I will see it all come true for me (Num. 11:23).

Thank you that you will perform more wonders and miracles than I can imagine (Job 9:10).

Thank you that you can do all things, and no plan of yours can be thwarted (Job 42:2).

Thank you that you made the earth, all people, and all animals on the earth, and you give it to anyone you please (Jer. 27:5).

Thank you that you can keep me from temptation and deliver me from Satan's power (Matt. 6:13).

Thank you that with you, all things are possible (Matt. 19:26).

Thank you that I am in error only when I don't know your power or your Word (Matt. 22:29).

Thank you that you can raise the dead—my dead body, my dead spirit, my dead mind, my dead emotions (Acts 26:8).

Thank you that someday in heaven there will be a multitude praising you for your salvation and glory and power (Rev. 19:1).

Supplication

Supplication

22

OMNIPRESENT

Adoration

Genesis 16:13: [Hagar] gave this name to the LORD who spoke to her: "You are the God who sees me," for she said, "I have now seen the One who sees me."

Genesis 28:16: Surely the LORD is in this place, and I was not aware of it.

Exodus 20:24: Make an altar of earth for me and sacrifice on it your burnt offerings and fellowship offerings, your sheep and goats and your cattle. Wherever I cause my name to be honored, I will come to you and bless you.

Psalm 139:3: You discern my going out and my lying down; you are familiar with all my ways.

Psalm 139:5: You hem me in—behind and before; you have laid your hand upon me.

Psalm 139:7–10: Where can I go from your Spirit? Where can I flee from your presence? If I go up to the heavens, you are there; if I make my bed in the depths, you are there. If I rise on the wings of the dawn, if I settle on the far side of the sea, even there your hand will guide me, your right hand will hold me fast.

Acts 17:24: The God who made the world and everything in it is the Lord of heaven and earth and does not live in temples built by hands.

Acts 17:27: God did this [see above passage] so that men would seek him and perhaps reach out for him and find him, though he is not far from each one of us.

1 Corinthians 12:6: There are different kinds of working, but the same God works all of them in all men.

Ephesians 1:23: [The church] is his body, the fullness of him who fills everything in every way.

Confession

Lord, forgive me when I think that I am alone. You are always near wherever I am, but I forget that. You also care for all people and are with all your children in any place. I ignore that often also, thinking that I must be there to help others when you can manage their lives perfectly well. Forgive my arrogance.

Thanksgiving

Thank you that you are everywhere and always near.
Thank you that you see me all the time (Gen. 16:13).
Thank you that you are in every place even when I am not aware of it (Gen. 28:16).
Thank you that you will come to me and bless me any-where I am as long as you are using me there to honor your name (Exod. 20:24).

Thank you that you know about everything that I do. You know when I go out and when I lie down (Ps. 139:3).

Thank you that you hem me in. I can't move without your being there because you have laid your hand upon me (Ps. 139:5).

Thank you that I can never get away from you. No matter where I go you are there, your hand always guiding and upholding me (Ps. 139:7–10).

Thank you that you don't live in temples or churches built by hands, but that you do live in my body because I am your child (Acts 17:24).

Thank you that when I seek you and reach out for you, I will find you because you are not far from me (Acts 17:27).

Thank you that you, the same God, can be in all men at the same time, giving each one different gifts (1 Cor. 12:6).

Thank you that you fill everything in every way (Eph. 1:23).

Supplication

Supplication

23

OMNISCIENT

Deuteronomy 2:7: The LORD your God has blessed you in all the work of your hands. He has watched over your journey through this vast desert. These forty years the LORD your God has been with you, and you have not lacked anything.

1 Chronicles 28:9: Acknowledge the God of your father, and serve him with wholehearted devotion and with a willing mind, for the LORD searches every heart and understands every motive behind the thoughts. If you seek him, he will be found by you; but if you forsake him, he will reject you forever.

Job 23:10: He knows the way that I take; when he has tested me, I will come forth as gold.

Psalm 139:2–4: You know when I sit and when I rise; you perceive my thoughts from afar. You discern my going out and my lying down; you are familiar with all my ways. Before a word is on my tongue you know it completely, O LORD.

Psalm 139:16: Your eyes saw my unformed body. All the days ordained for me were written in your book before one of them came to be.

Matthew 6:4: Your giving [should be done] in secret. Then your Father, who sees what is done in secret, will reward you.

Matthew 6:32: The pagans run after [food, drink, and clothing], and your heavenly Father knows that you need them.

Romans 8:29: Those God foreknew he also predestined to be conformed to the likeness of his Son, that he might be the firstborn among many brothers.

Romans 11:33: Oh, the depth of the riches of the wisdom and knowledge of God! How unsearchable his judgments, and his paths beyond tracing out!

Hebrews 4:13: Nothing in all creation is hidden from God's sight. Everything is uncovered and laid bare before the eyes of him to whom we must give account.

Confession

Lord, you know the way I take. Forgive me for not resting in that. You know my future and will lead me where I need to go. Forgive me for not resting in that. You also know my sins and have covered me with the righteousness of Jesus Christ. Forgive me for not thanking you every day for that.

Thanksgiving

Thank you for knowing all things.
Thank you that you have watched over me. You have been

with me all through my life, and I have not lacked anything (Deut. 2:7).

Thank you that you understand the motive behind every thought I have (1 Chron. 28:9).

Thank you that you know the way I take, and that when you test me, I will come forth as gold (Job 23:10).

Thank you that you are familiar with everything that I do. You know when I sit down, when I go to bed, and when I get up. You know my every thought, and before I even say a word, you know it (Ps. 139:2–4).

Thank you that you knew me before I was born, and that all the days ordained for me you had already decided (Ps. 139:16).

Thank you that those things that are done in secret will still be rewarded by you because you see them when nobody else does (Matt. 6:4).

Thank you that, as my heavenly Father, you know all the things I need, even the worldly kinds of things (Matt. 6:32).

Thank you that you foreknew me and predestined me to be conformed to the image of Jesus. Thank you that, eventually, I will become like Jesus (Rom. 8:29).

Thank you that the riches of your wisdom and knowledge are deep. Your judgments and ways are beyond me. Who could counsel you? (Rom. 11:33–34).

Thank you that nothing in all creation is hidden from your sight, and that some day I will have to give an account for all I have done or not done (Heb. 4:13).

Supplication

Supplication

24

PERFECT

Adoration

Deuteronomy 32:4: He is the Rock, his works are perfect, and all his ways are just. A faithful God who does no wrong, upright and just is he.

2 Samuel 22:31: As for God, his way is perfect; the word of the LORD is flawless. He is a shield for all who take refuge in him.

1 Kings 20:28: This is what the LORD says: "Because the Arameans think the LORD is a god of the hills and not a god of the valleys, I will deliver this vast army into your hands, and you will know that I am the LORD."

Isaiah 42:8: I am the LORD; that is my name! I will not give my glory to another or my praise to idols.

Matthew 5:48: Be perfect, therefore, as your heavenly Father is perfect.

John 17:3: This is eternal life: that they may know you, the only true God, and Jesus Christ, whom you have sent.

Romans 12:2: Do not conform any longer to the pattern of this world, but be transformed by the renewing of your mind. Then you will be able to test and approve what God's will is—his good, pleasing and perfect will.

1 Corinthians 8:4: About eating food sacrificed to idols: We know that an idol is nothing at all in the world and that there is no God but one.

1 Corinthians 8:6: For us there is but one God, the Father, from whom all things came and for whom we live; and there is but one Lord, Jesus Christ, through whom all things came and through whom we live.

James 1:17: Every good and perfect gift is from above, coming down from the Father of the heavenly lights, who does not change like shifting shadows.

Confession

Lord, you are perfect in all that you say and do, but I confess that I often question what you say and what you do. Please forgive me. You have told me that I am to be perfect even as you are perfect, and I fall so short of the mark. Usually I don't try or even think about it until after I have done something wrong. Please help me for your sake.

Thanksgiving

Thank you that I can count on your being perfect.
Thank you that all your works are perfect and all your
    ways are just (Deut. 32:4).
Thank you that your way is perfect—I can be sure of
    that—and your word is flawless. Therefore, when I am

in a struggle, my refuge will be in your way and your word (2 Sam. 22:31).

Thank you that those who do not believe that you are sufficient in every situation—not in just some situations—will fail (1 Kings 20:28).

Thank you that you will not give your glory to any other person (Isa. 42:8).

Thank you that you also want me to be perfect and that you are the standard (Matt. 5:48).

Thank you that eternal life is just knowing you and your Son Jesus Christ (John 17:3).

Thank you that you do not want me to live like the rest of the world, but to be transformed by the renewing of my mind, so that I will know what your will is for me (Rom. 12:2).

Thank you that idols have no value whatsoever (1 Cor. 8:4).

Thank you that everything comes from you—thus, I should live for you. Everything came through you—thus, I live only through you (1 Cor. 8:6).

Thank you that every good and perfect gift comes from you. You do not give me anything that is not good, because you do not change from being good and perfect (James 1:17).

Supplication

_____
_____
_____
_____
_____
_____
_____
_____
_____
_____
_____
_____
_____
_____
_____
_____
_____
_____
_____
_____
_____
_____
_____
_____
_____
_____
_____
_____
_____
_____

Supplication

25

PERSON

Adoration

Isaiah 45:5–6: I am the LORD, and there is no other; apart from me there is no God. I will strengthen you, though you have not acknowledged me, so that from the rising of the sun to the place of its setting men may know there is none besides me. I am the LORD, and there is no other.

Isaiah 46:5: To whom will you compare me or count me equal? To whom will you liken me that we may be compared?

Jeremiah 10:6: No one is like you, O LORD; you are great, and your name is mighty in power.

Jeremiah 14:22: Do any of the worthless idols of the nations bring rain? Do the skies themselves send down showers? No, it is you, O LORD our God. Therefore our hope is in you, for you are the one who does all this.

Jeremiah 32:27: I am the LORD, the God of all mankind. Is anything too hard for me?

Matthew 4:10: Jesus said to him, "Away from me, Satan! For it is written: 'Worship the Lord your God, and serve him only.'"

Matthew 23:9: Do not call anyone on earth "father," for you have one Father, and he is in heaven.

John 17:3: This is eternal life: that they may know you, the only true God, and Jesus Christ, whom you have sent.

Colossians 1:15: [The Son] is the image of the invisible God, the firstborn over all creation.

1 Timothy 2:5: There is one God and one mediator between God and men, the man Christ Jesus.

Confession

Lord, I confess that frequently I think of you as something other than a Person. Help me to realize that you are personal and care for me even when I do not acknowledge you.

Thanksgiving

Thank you that you, as a personal God, love me.

Thank you that you are the only God—no other god is personal and cares for me even when I do not acknowledge you or communicate with you as a person (Isa. 45:5–6).

Thank you that there is no other person who compares with you. No one is like you or equal to you (Isa. 46:5).

Thank you that you are also my Lord. You are the Lord of my flesh as well as the Lord of my spirit. None of my fleshly desires are too hard for you to handle (Jer. 10:6).

Thank you that you are the one who brings rain when we need it; it doesn't just happen. Therefore, my hope is in you, for you are the one who takes care of all my needs (Jer. 14:22).

Thank you that you are the Lord, the God of all mankind, and that nothing is too hard for you to do (Jer. 32:27).

Thank you that you have said I am to worship you only and serve you only (Matt. 4:10).

Thank you that I should never think of anyone else as my real father because you are my only true Father. You answer my needs from heaven (Matt. 23:9).

Thank you that knowing you and Jesus Christ, who was sent by you, is eternal life. Eternal life is wrapped up in your person (John 17:3).

Thank you that Jesus is the image of you, who are invisible. Jesus is you incarnate (Col. 1:15).

Thank you that although my sin separates me from you, there is a mediator between you and me—the man Jesus Christ (1 Tim. 2:5).

Supplication

Supplication

26

PRESERVER

Adoration

Psalm 116:6: The Lord protects the simplehearted; when I was in great need, he saved me.

Psalm 118:13: I was pushed back and about to fall, but the Lord helped me.

Psalm 145:14: The Lord upholds all those who fall and lifts up all who are bowed down.

Proverbs 3:6: In all your ways acknowledge [the Lord], and he will make your paths straight.

Isaiah 30:21: Whether you turn to the right or to the left, your ears will hear a voice behind you, saying, "This is the way; walk in it."

Matthew 10:29–31: Are not two sparrows sold for a penny? Yet not one of them will fall to the ground apart from the will of your Father. And even the very hairs of your head are all numbered. So don't be afraid; you are worth more than many sparrows.

Romans 8:28: In all things God works for the good of those who love him, who have been called according to his purpose.

1 Corinthians 10:13: No temptation has seized you except what is common to man. And God is faithful; he will not let you be tempted beyond what you can bear. But when you are tempted, he will also provide a way out so that you can stand up under it.

1 Peter 3:12–13: "The eyes of the Lord are on the righteous and his ears are attentive to their prayer, but the face of the Lord is against those who do evil." Who is going to harm you if you are eager to do good?

Revelation 3:10: Since you have kept my command to endure patiently, I will also keep you from the hour of trial that is going to come upon the whole world to test those who live on the earth.

Confession

Lord, too many times I have not acknowledged the way you have preserved me from harm. You have protected me again and again, and I have not thanked you for it. Frequently you have protected me from making stupid or deliberate errors. Forgive me for not giving you praise for it.

Thanksgiving

Thank you for preserving me all these years.
Thank you that you protect the simplehearted, and therefore, you save me when I am in great need (Ps. 116:6).
Thank you that when I am pushed back and about to fall, you will help me (Ps. 118:13).
Thank you that you uphold me when I fall and lift me up

when I am bowed down in humility or depression
(Ps. 145:14).

Thank you that when I acknowledge you in all my ways,
you will make my path straight (Prov. 3:6).

Thank you that no matter which way I try to turn, the
Holy Spirit will speak to me to keep me on the right
path (Isa. 30:21).

Thank you that you know when one little sparrow falls to
the ground, and that you have numbered even the
hairs on my head; I needn't be afraid that you won't
preserve me. I am worth a great deal to you (Matt.
10:29–31).

Thank you that in all things you are working for my good,
because I have been called by you according to your
purpose (Rom. 8:28).

Thank you that you will not let me be tempted beyond
what I can bear but will always provide a way out
(1 Cor. 10:13).

Thank you that, because you have made me righteous in
Christ Jesus, your eye is upon me and your ear is
attentive to my prayers. But you are against those who
do evil (1 Peter 3:12–13).

Thank you that when I keep your command to endure
patiently, you keep me from unnecessary trials and
testing (Rev. 3:10).

Supplication

Supplication

27

PROVIDER

Adoration

Job 22:24–25: Assign your nuggets to the dust, your gold of Ophir to the rocks in the ravines, then the Almighty will be your gold, the choicest silver for you.

Job 22:28: What you decide on will be done, and light will shine on your ways.

Psalm 23:1: The Lord is my shepherd, I shall not be in want.

Psalm 23:5–6: You prepare a table before me in the presence of my enemies. You anoint my head with oil; my cup overflows. Surely goodness and love will follow me all the days of my life, and I will dwell in the house of the Lord forever.

Psalm 34:9: Fear the Lord, you his saints, for those who fear him lack nothing.

Psalm 37:19: In times of disaster they will not wither; in days of famine they will enjoy plenty.

Zechariah 3:7: If you will walk in my ways and keep my requirements, then you will govern my house and have charge of my courts, and I will give you a place among these standing here.

Matthew 6:33: Seek first [the Father's] kingdom and his righteousness, and all these things will be given to you as well.

Luke 22:35: Then Jesus asked them, "When I sent you without purse, bag or sandals, did you lack anything?" "Nothing," they answered.

1 Corinthians 2:9: No eye has seen, no ear has heard, no mind has conceived what God has prepared for those who love him.

Confession

Lord, please forgive me for not always looking to you for my provision. I have tried to get what I need from others or do things for myself. You have always been there to provide for me, but I have not always trusted you to do so. You give me all that I need, and you are all that I need. Forgive me for not thanking you for your faithful provision.

Thanksgiving

Thank you for always providing for me.
Thank you that if I throw my own gold away, then you will be my gold and my silver (Job 22:24–25).
Thank you that having put desires in my heart, you let me decide what I want to do, and then you help me do it (Job 22:28).
Thank you that you are my shepherd. Therefore, I shall not be in want (Ps. 23:1).
Thank you that you give me a feast in front of all my enemies. You look after me and give to me abundantly.

Your goodness and mercy follow me all my life and in the life to come (Ps. 23:5–6).

Thank you that when I fear you enough to obey you, I will lack nothing that I need (Ps. 34:9).

Thank you that in times of disaster I will not wither and in days of famine I will enjoy plenty. You will see that I am cared for in the hard times (Ps. 37:19).

Thank you that if I walk in your ways and keep your requirements, then you will give me the place of leadership you want me to have (Zech. 3:7).

Thank you that if I seek your kingdom and your righteousness first, you will add everything to me that I need (Matt. 6:33).

Thank you that when you send me to do something— apparently without the equipment to provide for myself and my needs—I will find that I lack nothing (Luke 22:35).

Thank you that I have not seen or heard or even imagined what you have prepared for me just because I love you (1 Cor. 2:9).

Supplication

Supplication

28

RIGHTEOUS

Adoration

Numbers 23:19: God is not a man, that he should lie, nor a son of man, that he should change his mind. Does he speak and then not act? Does he promise and not fulfill?

Deuteronomy 32:4: He is the Rock, his works are perfect, and all his ways are just. A faithful God who does no wrong, upright and just is he.

Psalm 86:11: Teach me your way, O LORD, and I will walk in your truth; give me an undivided heart, that I may fear your name.

Psalm 119:144: Your statutes are forever right; give me understanding that I may live.

Psalm 143:1: O LORD, hear my prayer, listen to my cry for mercy; in your faithfulness and righteousness come to my relief.

Psalm 145:17: The LORD is righteous in all his ways and loving toward all he has made.

Matthew 6:33: Seek first [the Father's] kingdom and his righteousness, and all these things will be given to you as well.

John 17:17: Sanctify them by the truth; your word is truth.

2 Timothy 4:8: There is in store for me the crown of righteousness, which the Lord, the righteous Judge, will award to me on that day—and not only to me, but also to all who have longed for his appearing.

2 Peter 1:1: To those who through the righteousness of our God and Savior Jesus Christ have received a faith as precious as ours.

Confession

Lord, when I meditate on your righteousness, I realize how far short I fall. Forgive me for my self-righteousness and for thinking for even a moment that my self-righteousness is true righteousness. Self-righteousness is pride, and I confess that I am full of it. I repent and will from this day forward seek only the practical righteousness that comes from living in obedience to you. Please forgive me, too, for not thanking you daily for the righteousness of Jesus Christ that you have freely given me in your grace.

Thanksgiving

Thank you for giving me your righteousness.
Thank you that you never make a promise you don't fulfill (Num. 23:19).
Thank you that you are my Rock; your words are the right words for me; your ways are the right ways for me. You will be faithful to me because you do no wrong and are always right (Deut. 32:4).
Thank you that you want me to be righteous, too. You

will teach me your ways so that I can walk in your truths, and you will give me an undivided heart that I may fear your name (Ps. 86:11).

Thank you that your statutes are forever right, and you will give me understanding of them that I may live (Ps. 119:144).

Thank you that you hear my prayer, that you listen when I cry for mercy, that in your faithfulness and righteousness you will come to my relief (Ps. 143:1).

Thank you that you are righteous in all your ways and that you are loving toward all you have made. That means me as well as all creation (Ps. 145:17).

Thank you for telling me that, to be holy in your eyes, I am to seek first your kingdom—that is, to demonstrate your righteousness by doing those things that are your will for me in bringing others to you. Then you will give me everything else; there is nothing I need to seek for myself (Matt. 6:33).

Thank you that I am sanctified by truth and your word is truth (John 17:17).

Thank you that there is a crown of righteousness awaiting me if I long for your appearing (2 Tim. 4:8).

Thank you that I have received the gift of faith, which is as precious as that given to anyone else. It is the same faith as given to the great figures in Scripture (2 Peter 1:1).

Supplication

Supplication

29

SAVIOR

Deuteronomy 32:39: I myself am He! There is no god besides me. I put to death and I bring to life, I have wounded and I will heal, and no one can deliver out of my hand.

Psalm 27:1: The LORD is my light and my salvation—whom shall I fear? The LORD is the stronghold of my life—of whom shall I be afraid?

Psalm 34:22: The LORD redeems his servants; no one will be condemned who takes refuge in him.

Psalm 50:23: He who sacrifices thank offerings honors me, and he prepares the way so that I may show him the salvation of God.

Psalm 68:19: Praise be to the Lord, to God our Savior, who daily bears our burdens.

John 3:16–17: God so loved the world that he gave his one and only Son, that whoever believes in him shall not perish but have eternal life. For God did not send his Son into the world to condemn the world, but to save the world through him.

Romans 8:31: If God is for us, who can be against us?

1 Corinthians 1:18: The message of the cross is foolishness to those who are perishing, but to us who are being saved it is the power of God.

2 Timothy 1:9: [God] has saved us and called us to a holy life—not because of anything we have done but because of his own purpose and grace. This grace was given us in Christ Jesus before the beginning of time.

Titus 2:11: The grace of God that brings salvation has appeared to all men.

Confession

Lord, I have not sacrificed many thank offerings to you for the salvation you have extended to me in your grace. Forgive me. So many times you have saved me from the world, the flesh, and the Devil, and I have not even been aware of it. Forgive me. Many ways I have not trusted you to save me when salvation was available. Forgive me. Mostly, forgive me for not considering deeply what it cost Jesus to save me.

Thanksgiving

Thank you for saving me.
Thank you that you are the one who puts to death and who brings to life. You wound and you heal (Deut. 32:39).
Thank you that you are my light, so why should I be

afraid of anyone? Thank you that you are the strength of my life; therefore I need fear no one (Ps. 27:1).

Thank you that I will not be condemned when I take refuge in you because you redeem your servants (Ps. 34:22).

Thank you that you use my thank offerings to prepare the way to show me your salvation (Ps. 50:23).

Thank you that you daily bear my burdens—they are no longer mine to carry (Ps. 68:19).

Thank you that you loved me enough to give your one and only Son so that I can have eternal life and not be condemned (John 3:16–17).

Thank you that if you are for me it doesn't matter who is against me (Rom. 8:31).

Thank you that I experience salvation each day as I apply the message of the Cross to my life. Thank you that salvation releases your power in my life (1 Cor. 1:18).

Thank you that you have a purpose for my life (2 Tim. 1:9).

Thank you that your saving grace will appear to me today (Titus 2:11).

Supplication

Supplication

30

SOVEREIGN

Adoration

1 Chronicles 29:12: Wealth and honor come from you; you are the ruler of all things. In your hands are strength and power to exalt and give strength to all.

2 Chronicles 20:6: O LORD, God of our fathers, are you not the God who is in heaven? You rule over all the kingdoms of the nations. Power and might are in your hand, and no one can withstand you.

Job 41:11: [And the LORD said to Job,] "Who has a claim against me that I must pay? Everything under heaven belongs to me."

Psalm 75:6–7: No one from the east or the west or from the desert can exalt a man. But it is God who judges: He brings one down, he exalts another.

Isaiah 45:7: I form the light and create darkness, I bring prosperity and create disaster; I, the LORD, do all these things.

Isaiah 45:23: By myself I have sworn, my mouth has uttered in all integrity a word that will not be revoked: Before me every knee will bow; by me every tongue will swear.

Matthew 11:25: I praise you, Father, Lord of heaven and earth, because you have hidden these things from the wise and learned, and revealed them to little children.

Matthew 20:15: Don't I [the Lord/landowner] have the right to do what I want with my own money? Or are you envious because I am generous?

John 10:29: My Father, who has given [my sheep] to me, is greater than all; no one can snatch them out of my Father's hand.

Acts 17:26: From one man he made every nation of men, that they should inhabit the whole earth; and he determined the times set for them and the exact places where they should live.

Confession

Forgive me, Lord, for wanting to be sovereign over myself. Instead of wanting you to be sovereign, I have wanted my own way, acting as if I have a right to my own life. I have rebelled against your authority, and I repent, joyously accepting that you are my Master.

Thanksgiving

Thank you for being sovereign over the world and me.
Thank you that wealth and honor come from you
(1 Chron. 29:12).
Thank you that you rule over all nations and no one can
withstand you. I need not worry about what will
happen in the political world (2 Chron. 20:6).

Thank you that everything under heaven belongs to you (Job 41:11).

Thank you that no one can exalt a person—only you. You are the judge and you bring one down and exalt another (Ps. 75:6–7).

Thank you that you create light and darkness, prosperity and disaster. You are the Lord and you do all these things (Isa. 45:7).

Thank you that some day every knee will bow before you and every tongue will confess you as Lord (Isa. 45:23).

Thank you that you hide things from the wise and learned, but reveal them to little children. Therefore, when I depend upon you as a child would, you will reveal things to me, too (Matt. 11:25).

Thank you that you have a right to do what you want with your own money. I have no right to be envious if you want to be generous with another person. Everything belongs to you (Matt. 20:15).

Thank you that since you have given me to Jesus, no one can snatch me out of his hand (John 10:29).

Thank you that you determine the times set for every person and the exact places where they should live (Acts 17:26).

Supplication

Supplication

31

WISE

Adoration

Exodus 4:11–12: Who gave man his mouth? Who makes him deaf or mute? Who gives him sight or makes him blind? Is it not I, the LORD? Now go; I will help you speak and will teach you what to say.

Job 9:4: His wisdom is profound, his power is vast. Who has resisted him and come out unscathed?

Job 12:13: To God belong wisdom and power; counsel and understanding are his.

Job 12:16: To him belong strength and victory; both deceived and deceiver are his.

Psalm 104:24: How many are your works, O LORD! In wisdom you made them all; the earth is full of your creatures.

Daniel 2:20–22: Praise be to the name of God for ever and ever; wisdom and power are his. He changes times and seasons; he sets up kings and deposes them. He gives wisdom to the wise and knowledge to the discerning. He reveals deep and hidden things; he knows what lies in darkness, and light dwells with him.

Romans 16:27: To the only wise God be glory forever through Jesus Christ! Amen.

1 Corinthians 1:24–25: To those whom God has called, both Jews and Greeks, Christ the power of God and the wisdom of God. For the foolishness of God is wiser than man's wisdom, and the weakness of God is stronger than man's strength.

Ephesians 1:8: He lavishe[s] on us with all wisdom and understanding.

Ephesians 3:10: His intent was that now, through the church, the manifold wisdom of God should be made known to the rulers and authorities in the heavenly realms.

Confession

Lord, forgive me for relying upon my own wisdom when yours is readily available. I have not always sought your guidance. I have frequently looked to the world for counsel instead of looking into your Word. I repent and ask you to help me look only to you for all the wisdom that I will ever need.

Thanksgiving

Thank you for supplying your wisdom to me whenever I need it.

Thank you that you are the one who gave me my mouth to speak, my ears to hear, and my eyes to see. Therefore, I can trust you to help me speak when you want me to and to teach me what to say (Exod. 4:11–12).

Thank you that your wisdom is deep and you have the
power to back it up (Job 9:4).

Thank you that your counsel is best for me (Job 12:13).

Thank you that to you belong strength and victory; you
know and control those who are deceived as well as
those who deceive others (Job 12:16).

Thank you that the earth is full of your works—every
animal, plant, and rock—and that all your works are
made in your wisdom (Ps. 104:24).

Thank you that you give wisdom to the wise and knowledge to the discerning. You reveal deep and hidden
things because you know what lies in darkness
(Dan. 2:20–22).

Thank you that you only are wise and you are glorified
through Jesus Christ, so as I love, honor, and obey
Jesus I glorify you (Rom. 16:27).

Thank you that since I am called by you, Christ is my
power and my wisdom, and even his foolishness is
wiser than any wisdom I could bring forth on my own
(1 Cor. 1:24–25).

Thank you that you have lavished upon me your wisdom
and understanding (Eph. 1:8).

Thank you that your intent is that, through the church—
which is your body—your wisdom is to be shown to
the Devil and his followers (Eph. 3:10).

Supplication

Supplication

My Personal Insights

My Personal Insights

My Personal Insights

My Personal Insights

My Personal Insights

My Personal Insights

My Personal Insights

My Personal Insights